MOODS OF
STAFFORDSHIRE

VAN GREAVES

HALSGROVE

First published in Great Britain in 2007

Title page photograph: *The Upper Dove Valley seen near Longnor*

British Library Cataloguing-in-Publication Data
A CIP record for this title is available from the British Library

ISBN 1 84114 528 9
ISBN 978 1 84114 528 0

HALSGROVE
Halsgrove House
Ryelands Farm Industrial Estate,
Bagley Green, Wellington,
Somerset TA21 9PZ
email: sales@halsgrove.com
website: www.halsgrove.com

Printed and bound by D'Auria Industrie Grafiche, Italy

INTRODUCTION

This brief journey through the deceptively-large and infinitely-varied county of Staffordshire shows it through the discerning eye of the photographer. Staffordshire's long, thin southern arm adjoins Worcestershire, then skirts around the Black Country portion of the West Midlands, providing a fascinating mix of pretty countryside with elements of industrial heritage, including many of the sleepy canals which abound throughout the county.

To the north lies the quiet, flat rural country west of the M6, dotted with charming villages, while to the east, suburban towns and villages surround Cannock Chase, a former hunting-ground of kings and now a remnant of birch and heather-covered heathland. This is a walkers' haven which includes managed conifer plantations in many parts.

To the east of here, the lack of outstanding natural features is compensated for by the lure of historic Lichfield, with a stunningly-ornate three-spired cathedral as its centrepiece. Other towns include the Saxon capital of Tamworth, with its red sandstone castle, and the brewery town of Burton upon Trent. Between the two lies the newly-created National Memorial Arboretum and part of the National Forest.

Looking west, the market town of Uttoxeter is of Saxon origin, and the county town of Stafford is both architecturally and culturally stimulating. On the northern tip of Cannock Chase stands eighteenth-century Shugborough Hall, a popular tourist attraction now in the hands of the National Trust and the home, until his recent death, of photographer Lord Patrick Lichfield.

The M6 corridor brings us to Stoke on Trent and the Potteries, the birthplace of English ceramics, and home to such famous names as Spode, Wedgwood, Burleigh and Moorland. The original skyline of the five Potteries towns was once punctuated with the distinctive shapes of bottle kilns, and though many have disappeared, thankfully a few have been preserved.

North and east of the Potteries grand countryside prevails as the land rises to the Staffordshire Moorlands, a region of gritstone crags and escarpments falling away to gloriously-wooded dales. The classic defile of the Churnet Valley is threaded by a preserved steam railway and, mercifully, the modern white-knuckle rides of Alton Towers – Britain's biggest theme park – contrive to remain hidden in the surrounding estate's wooded flanks.

We climb yet again to the Weaver Hills, and up onto the White (limestone) Peak of the south-western corner of the Peak District National Park. This is dominated by the Dove and Manifold Valleys, and proudly accentuated in the west by the famous gritstone outcrops of Hen Cloud and The Roaches and the rugged Dane Valley, terminating the county at remote Three Shires Head.

Staffordshire is an underrated county which is certainly worthy of more detailed exploration. I hope this collection of photographs will tempt the reader to do just that.

Van Greaves, Spring, 2007

Key
······· National Park boundary
--- National Forest boundary
━━━ County boundary

PEAK DISTRICT
NATIONAL PARK

Tittesworth
Reservoir

Rudyard
Reservoir

• Biddulph

LEEK

CHESHIRE

NEWCASTLE-
UNDER-LYME

STOKE-
ON-TRENT

Caldon Canal

Stoke

• Cheadle

Trentham •

DERBYSHIRE

STONE

UTTOXETER

Eccleshall •

STAFFORDSHIRE

Tutbury •

Blithfield
Reservoir

BURTON
UPON TRENT

Aqualate
Mere

STAFFORD

Shropshire Union Canal

Trent & Mersey Canal

SHROPSHIRE

Belvide
Reservoir

RUGELEY

CANNOCK

LICHFIELD

Chase
water

TAMWORTH

Codsall •

Shenstone •

N
W   E
S

WARWICKSHIRE

• Wombourne

BIRMINGHAM

LOCATION MAP

STOURBRIDGE

Winter dawn, The Roaches looking towards Shutlingsloe
This is one of my favourite Peak District views. The intriguing summit rocks of The Roaches could yield any number of compositions. The time of day and the conditions were the determining factor in this case. Shutlingsloe, a mini mountain over 1600 feet (500 metres) high, is in Cheshire across the Dane Valley which forms the county boundary.

Sundown, The Roaches and Hen Cloud from Tittesworth Reservoir
This and the next picture are what greeted me looking either side of the road bridge which spans the reservoir, north of Leek. Sometimes a rich light is reflected from gritstone, a normally brown, dingy-coloured sedimentary rock.

Sundown, Tittesworth Reservoir
The reflection of the cloud is particularly attractive.
The light and colour add mystique to what might have been a bland scene in normal daylight.

Staffordshire & Worcestershire Canal at Kinver
Canal users enjoy a picturesque section of the waterway.

Negotiating Bratch Locks, on the Staffordshire & Worcestershire Canal
A narrowboat negotiates the locks on another delightful section of the canal, near Wombourne close to Wolverhampton.

Moseley Old Hall

Elizabethan Moseley Old Hall, near Wolverhampton, is known as the house that saved a king. Charles II is said to have hidden here in a priest hole in this property, now in the hands of the National Trust.

Weston Park
This superb seventeenth-century stately home near the Shropshire border is set in 1000 acres of 'Capability' Brown landscaped parkland. It has a magnificent interior and is known these days for its events, particularly outdoor concerts.

Longnor from the south
This former market town set inside the Staffordshire Moorlands part of the Peak District was a
former playground of mine. I used to stay with other climbing friends in the vicarage occupied then by the
parents of one of our group. Many an oatcake and many a beer were consumed in those happy times.

Thor's Cave, Manifold Valley and Grindon Church
The spirit of an English summer's morning is captured in this image.
I hope, like me, it makes you want to be there. The setting is in the heart of the Staffordshire Peak.

Ancient High House, Stafford
This is the largest timber-framed town house in England, built in 1595.
It contains the Museum of the Staffordshire Yeomanry.

Ford Green Hall, Stoke on Trent
This richly-furnished seventeenth-century house is now a museum which holds regular events.
It is captured here in quiet, autumnal mode.

Snow on drystone walls near Flash
If you study this picture, you will see there is one gritstone
wall in front of another. The gap between in this
foreshortened picture is an ancient 'green lane'.

Birchenclough, near Flash
The drystone walls come into their own in this winter moorland study.

Butter Market, Leek
This is a fine example of a
Victorian indoor market. Most of
these have sadly disappeared...
not for the better.

Market Square, Leek
There are some proud towns with proud buildings in Staffordshire, and this is one of them.

Stepping Stones, Sherbrook Valley, Cannock Chase
Cannock Chase is designated as an Area of Outstanding Natural Beauty (AONB),
and the tree-cloaked valley of the Sherbrook is one of its most attractive places and a
beautiful picnic site. Walking on the chase is popular along easy graded tracks.

From Kinver Edge to the Clent Hills
Colourful autumn birches grace the foreground in this view from Staffordshire into Worcestershire.

Dorothy Clive Garden
These lovely gardens are a popular place to visit near Blackbrook on the A51.
This image captures a seemingly natural corner of this varied and pretty garden.

Island Pool, Baggeridge Country Park
Sited on the remains of a former Black Country colliery, there are several pools in this undulating dell.
Now completely reclaimed by nature. Island Pool is arguably the finest example.

Ancient Buttercross and the Goat Inn, Abbots Bromley

The buttercross dates from 1339, a time when Abbots Bromley was an important market town. The inn got its name from the goats said to be given to Sir John Bagot (from a Norman family associated with the town) by Richard II for his hunting.

Abbots Bromley Horn Dance
This ancient event dates back at least to the eleventh century and takes place on Wakes Monday,
after the first Sunday in September. It moves to several venues around the town and surrounding farms.
The horns, said to be from reindeer, are usually kept in the parish church.

Lock-up in Alton
This and the next picture are examples of village lock-ups from bygone times. Both are small, but quite different in character.

Lock-up in Gnosall
This example has been moved from its original site and placed as we see it here.

Cow in the River Dane at Gradbach

Cow and Ipstones
It is common to see black-and-white Friesian dairy cows in Staffordshire.
Ipstones is a Staffordshire Moorlands' village north of the Churnet Valley at about 780 ft/240m above sea level.

**Winking Eye Buttress,
Ramshaw Rocks**
I could have timed this picture
to have light and detail in the 'face'
in the rocks. Instead I waited for the
sun to go behind the castellated
rocks of this gritstone outcrop
adjacent to the A53 north of Leek,
creating a more graphic image.

Ramshaw Rocks
Here, I've tried to illustrate the general tilt of the rocks.
Note the pinnacle at the far end and the A53 as it undulates south towards Leek.

**Sir Peter Walker's Maltings,
Clarence Street, Burton upon Trent**
Built in 1884, this is a rare example
of an octagonal brew house.
It wasn't viable for long as so much
residue was left in the corners.
It is due for conversion into
apartments.

Bottle Kiln, Moorland Pottery Museum, Burslem
The Potteries' skyline was once filled with these distinctive buildings. Thankfully, though many have disappeared, several like this one have been preserved. Note the two pigeons perched half way up.

Shugborough Hall

The rear view of the hall, seen here, is not as widely published as the front elevation. Apart from the main entrance's fine portals, the gardens at the rear make for a more pictorial foreground. Sadly, the former owner, Lord Patrick Lichfield, famous photographer and cousin of the Queen, passed away suddenly at the end of 2005.

Tamworth Castle
Viewed from across the River Tame, this is one of Britain's most intact Norman shell keeps, with apartments including a haunted room and great hall and with exhibits dating from the twelfth to the nineteenth centuries.

Enville Church
This and the next picture are examples of churches at each end of Staffordshire. St Mary's at Enville is a rich
red sandstone church with an elegant design, owing much to the restoration by George Gilbert Scott in 1872-5.

Church of the Holy Cross, Ilam
The church contains a chapel with a shrine to the Saxon Saint Bertelin, which was a site of pilgrimage.
Beyond are the first hills of the Peak District.

Gnosall
Note the old looking thatched roofed building on the left of this view of the main street of the west Staffordshire village of Gnosall. You could mistake it for Tudor, but in fact it is Victorian.

Brewood Village centre

Not many miles from Wolverhampton, Brewood (pronounced 'Brood') shows off its mainly Georgian village centre.

Stepping stones, Dovedale
Pictured from the Staffordshire side of the River Dove, the accessibility and
popularity in summer of this lovely corner of the Peak District are very apparent.

Leaving Hall Dale for Stanhope
In contrast to the previous shot, this confirms the impression that solitude can
be gained even within the much-frequented Peak District National Park.

Winter overlook of Roche Grange

As seen from the summit of The Roaches. The spelling of this farm complex is different, and older, than the usual one for the nearby gritstone edge. This and the next composition are telephoto shots with no sky, allowing the land and vegetation patterns to dominate.

Lonely barn in the Churnet Valley
An isolated building surrounded by autumnal trees.

Bratch Pumping Station
This old water pumping station for the South Staffordshire Waterworks has four ornamental turrets and includes a working steam engine.

Whitfield Colliery, Fegg Hayes, the Potteries
This is a country park adjacent to the former North Staffordshire Coalfield colliery.
I climbed a reclaimed slag heap to gain this overlook.

A house dating from 1560 in Kinver's High Street

Wightwick Manor
On the edge of Wolverhampton and looking every bit a Tudor manor house, Wightwick Manor
is in fact Victorian, dating from 1887. The house, now run by the National Trust, was designed by
Edward Ould for Theodore Mander with an interior by William Morris and C. E. Kempe.

Towards the Conservatory, Weston Park
If you venture to the rear of the main building of Weston Park you will find this landscaped
pool, and through the flowers, catch a glimpse of a greenhouse with exotic plants.

**The Queen's Gardens,
Newcastle under Lyme**
In the town centre of Newcastle
is this small garden with its
statue of Queen Victoria, which
gives it its name. It features a
beautiful array of flowers
in the summer months.

Biddulph Grange
James Bateman, a wealthy Manchester industrialist, created this series of compartments and landscaped gardens
over a sixteen-year period in the mid nineteenth century. His interest in botany led him to obtain plants
from all over the world. Biddulph Grange is now managed by the National Trust.

Himley Hall
The pools of Baggeridge Country Park feed the grounds of this Palladian mansion,
once the seat of the Earl of Dudley. It replaced a medieval mansion on the same site.

Wings of Unreason, The Roaches

'Wings of Unreason' is the name of one of the modern rock climbing 'problems' on the climbers' playground of The Roaches. The climbing involves a very 'thin' section of steep slab. The crux of the climb near the top forces the climber to leap up for the square-cut hold with little take-off purchase for his feet and, in one movement, 'mantleshelf' over the lip of the crag to finish.

Moon over Hen Cloud
Hen Cloud's buttresses, another playground for the rock climber, glow warm in evening light,
with an evocative moon hung in the sky above.

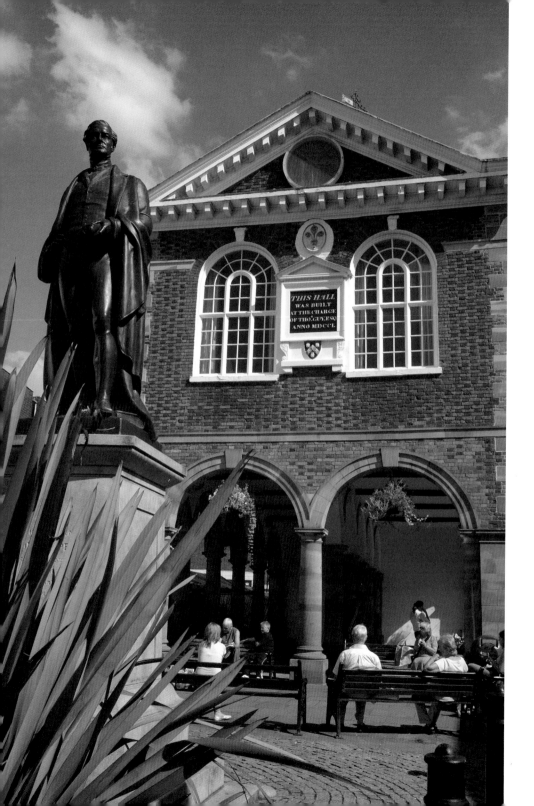

**Sir Robert Peel statue
and Town Hall, Tamworth**
Robert Peel (1788-1850) was the
MP for Tamworth and the
founder of the Metropolitan Police.
The town hall was built by
Thomas Guy in 1701, and is
the site of a market. The space
under the arches has also
been used for storage of an
old fire engine, and it has been
sandbagged as an air raid shelter
during the Second World War.

Conduit, Millennium Monument and Market Place, Uttoxeter
There is a tablet in the stone of the conduit with two dates referring to the
famous eighteenth century lexicographer, Dr Samuel Johnson, a Staffordshire man.

River Dove at Ellastone
The Staffordshire Way forms
a riverside walk along
pleasant meadows at Ellastone.

River Sow at Shugborough
You can walk from the famous hall though the grounds to this point where, in the picture,
children are playing on a warm summer's day.

Lonely barn near Alstonefield, Staffordshire Peak

The composition is simplistic with just a tree and interesting cloud to balance the barn, whose angles catch the attractive light.

Marsh Marigolds and barn at Lower Elkstone, Staffordshire Peak
I took up a very low angle to illustrate the flowers, backed by a typical stone-built barn of the area.

Trent & Mersey Canal, Alrewas
This and the next picture provide rural and urban contrasts to the Staffordshire network of canals.

Longport dry dock and canal basin, the Potteries

Church and cooling towers, Rugeley

There are times when you have to search for pictures. I saw the possibilities of the juxtaposition of the two entirely different architectural forms, but I ended up walking half-way round Rugeley to find the right angle.

**Rugeley Power Station
from Castle Ring, Cannock Chase**
The convenient hole in the
attractive trees gave me the
pleasing image seen here. I was
perched on a steep slope of
these Iron Age earthworks
with the tripod, dicing with
friction and gravity to obtain
the best composition.

Market Square, Burton upon Trent
A summer evening after the shops have closed gives both quieter streets and a warmer light.

Coors Brewery, Burton upon Trent
The factory may be environmentally unfriendly, but it is vital to economics of the town.

Highgate Common
Frequented by trippers from the Black Country, this heathland common has attractive walking and picnic areas.
The storm cloud beyond reminds me of a bomb explosion.

Enville sheepwalks
This and the previous shot show countryside close to the Black Country conurbation.
Turners Hill at Rowley Regis provides the background.

National Memorial Arboretum near Alrewas
This 150-acre site between Lichfield and Burton upon Trent is for the remembrance
of those who have suffered or lost their lives in service to this country.

Chinese Garden, Biddulph Grange
This is a particular feature of the gardens of Biddulph Grange,
inspired by the ideas of its original owner, James Bateman.

Dale Bottom, near Milldale, Staffordshire Peak
This isolated cottage with its flower garden is a picture in summer.

Milldale
On the Staffordshire side of the River Dove, this hamlet is best seen from the Derbyshire side.

Winter graveyard, Flash
There is a 'Bronte' feel to this bleak cemetery at 1500 feet/457m above sea level.

German War Cemetery, Cannock Chase
Look carefully and the names on the stones say the rest.
A memorial to the Germans who died in this country during two World Wars.

Pair of Small Pearl Bordered Fritillaries, Sherbrook Valley, Cannock Chase
These beautiful butterflies were photographed on one of those sultry evenings when thunderstorms
might brew. Consequently, the lack of sun made them inactive and easier to capture on film.

Grass Snake on vegetation on River Stour, Kinver
Spotted when crossing the road bridge over this tributary to the River Severn, the reptile
basked in the afternoon sun before swimming off to the bank. Note the yellow spot
by the neck of the snake, which is a good identification mark.

Winter tree, Kinver Edge
Is global warming making these conditions rare? I think they probably are.
Who knows, shots like this might be collectors' items in years to come.

Kinver Edge overlook
The sandstone edge is not much over 400 feet/122m above sea level but, where the trees part, there are gorgeous views over the birch woods which provide as good an advert for England's countryside as anywhere.

Grey Heron fishing at Walk Mill
This was an opportunist shot. I was looking originally to use the mill as a whole, but then
spotted one of the most graceful of British birds, seen here below a bank of daffodils.

Squirrel and jackdaw on a Gnosall roof.
The intrigue of still and real life is added to here by the thatched
roof and the half moon in another opportunist photograph
taken in this west Staffordshire village.

Small farmhouses near Winnothdale, Staffordshire Moorlands
Hereabouts the field enclosures are small, and each dwelling would
have been a separate farm two centuries ago.

The Peak from The Cloud, Bosley
The Cloud is an outlying hill of the Peak District. I am standing in Staffordshire although a few feet behind me lies Cheshire.
The turreted hill on the horizon is Shutlingsloe, again in Cheshire. The sheet of water is Bosley Reservoir.

Stafford Castle
The Norman motte and bailey castle with hall keep dates from 1348. What was left after the Civil War was given a Gothic reconstruction. It stands proud on a conical hill outside the town, a landmark on the M6 motorway.

A view of Tutbury Castle
Part of the Duchy of Lancaster's Needwood Estate, this eleventh-century fortress is well-situated on a hill surrounded by woodland. It is almost impossible to photograph as a whole, so this is just a section.

Daffodils and St Mary's Church, Colton
This was taken on a typical April day, as can be seen by the threatening sky behind the church,
which is situated on a village green near Rugeley.

A corner of Church Eaton
This picture of the quiet village in western Staffordshire features a car, which gives
a sense of modernity in a place that could otherwise be timeless.

Moortop Lodge
This fine dwelling was seen on a walk across parkland near the Weaver Hills.

Brookley's Lake
The JCB (Bamford's) testing track circumnavigates this man-made lake near Alton, photographed here in the autumn.

Nether Coleshaw Farm, Staffordshire Peak District
Drystone walls are a wonderful feature of the upland English landscape.
I was particularly satisfied with this pattern with the farm as the focal point.

Coleshaw area to Axe Edge
Photographers often develop themes, none more so than myself in this example, where the farm in
the previous picture now falls into the middle distance and the watching sheep hold the gaze.

Gritstone shapes
I scrambled among the rocks of Upper Tier of The Roaches to find this dramatic view through to Hen Cloud.

Ramshaw Rocks from The Roaches
This illustrates the rugged nature of 'Dark Peak' gritstone moorland country.

Carrdale, Longnor
The picture shows the dwelling used in the TV series *Peak Practice*. ('Carrdale' is of course a fictitious name.)

Jack Thompson of Longnor
Jack Thompson, a local character, was born and bred in Longnor.

Blithfield Reservoir and cooling towers, Rugeley Power Station
Where land undulations are gentle as hereabouts in Staffordshire, it is essential to
find the best compositional lines and somewhere on which to rest the eye.

Dusk, River Trent and Rugeley Power Station
While the power station might be said by some to be an eyesore, its cooling towers certainly dominate the surrounding landscape, and thus feature more than once in this book.

Izaak Walton's Cottage, Shallowford
The dwelling is now a museum dedicated to the man who co-wrote *The Compleat Angler*, the seventeenth-century angling classic.

Cave houses, Kinver

The homes were hewn out of the red sandstone rock, and the last occupant only left in the 1960s. Recently, some have been restored and are now under the management of the National Trust, and open to the public on certain days.

Shropshire Union Canal at Wheaton Aston
Some elder statesmen put the world to rights on the canal side.

Fradley Junction
This popular canal mooring site is situated near Lichfield at the junction of the Trent & Mersey and Coventry Canals.

WEDGWOOD

Display stand at Wedgwood Visitor Centre, Barlaston
This and the next picture are examples of collections from famous pottery firms, past and present.

Opposite:
Jugs from the Blue Italian Collection, Spode Factory Shop, Stoke

Mere behind Betley
These lakes are remnants of glacial action from the last Ice Age. They are found in Cheshire, Staffordshire and Shropshire.
This one has no name on the map and is east of the A531 and just north of the village of Betley, near the Cheshire boundary.

Betley Mere
This is the lake situated in gentle rolling country to the south west of the village of Betley.

**Towards Alstonefield
from near Wetton**
There is nothing like limestone
walls – surely one of man's kindest
additions to the British
landscape – to accentuate
the scenery.

Butterton

The finest view of this Staffordshire Peakland village is from the south, as its buildings spread down the hill from the church.

Cheddleton Flint Mill
I had driven past this easily-missed site a number of times without noticing it.
There has been a mill here since the thirteenth century. It was a corn mill in 1694,
but the need to grind flint (used to whiten pottery) arose about 1718.

Gradbach Mill
A youth hostel since 1980, this beautifully-situated mill is on the banks of the River Dane. Built in 1775,
it replaced an original mill of 1640 destroyed by fire. It was used for the manufacture of sewing silk,
but went into decline and disuse when water-power ceased to be economical.

The Old Man of Mow
This is an isolated gritstone pillar left in a quarry, enjoying a fine outlook
and standing a few hundred yards from the folly of Mow Cop.

Lud's Church, The Roaches
This is the antithesis of the previous picture. This strange chasm in Back Forest north of The Roaches gets its name from a medieval follower of John Wycliff, or possibly from the Luddites. It was formed by a landslip, and is pretty much a one-off feature in the millstone grit landscape.

Cheadle view
Seen from the east near Highshutt on a glorious summer's day, Cheadle stands comfortably in an otherwise rural setting.

Leek and Tittesworth Reservoir from The Roaches
Again, the use of a telephoto lens foreshortens the landscape.

Wall Roman site *(Letocetum)*
These are the foundations of a Roman army post on the A5 Watling Street
near Lichfield, which include a bathhouse and an inn.

Mow Cop Folly

It is said that 10,000 people attended the first Primitive Methodist gathering on this site in 1807. It was built as a 'castle ruin' in 1754 for Randle Wilbraham I of Rode Hall, and stands at 1096ft/334 metres above sea level, commanding 360 degree views. I have illustrated it here as if it is growing out of the gritstone outcrop on which it stands.

**Lichfield Cathedral
from Memorial Garden**
Built between 1195 and the 1330s,
the present building is the third
on the site, replacing previous
Saxon and Norman churches.
One of Britain's smaller cathedrals,
its three spires, the tallest
of which is 252ft/77m high,
are a distinctive feature.
(The garden is also known as
The Garden of Rememberance).

The Screen
Lichfield Cathedral Interior

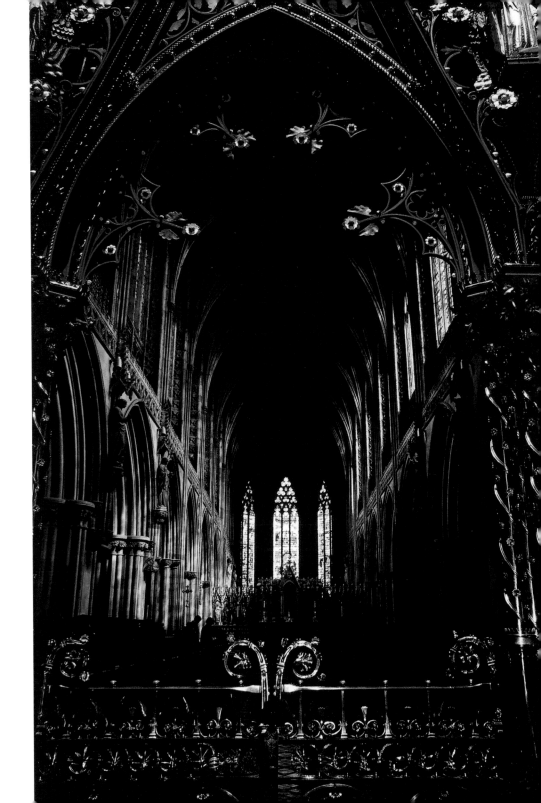

High Street, Eccleshall
An endearing feature of
this small town is this row
of arches supporting the
buildings above.

High Street, Stone
Modern additions have been sympathetically matched with older Georgian buildings on this pedestrianised street.

Tree and Hen Cloud
I never tire of this picture, which is balanced by two contrasting subjects, the tree and the hill, with added attractive cloud.

Parkhouse Hill, Earl Sterndale and the River Dove from Hollinsclough Moor
The viewpoint is just inside Staffordshire. Beyond the River Dove most of the
subject matter, including shapely Parkhouse Hill, is in Derbyshire.

On the Barlaston Estate
The beauty of this man-made lake and bridge is accentuated by springtime blossom.

From the Duke of Sutherland's Monument, Trentham Gardens
The gardens have recently undergone a facelift, and there is now a large monkey enclosure on site.
The best view is from the stiff walk uphill to the monument, from where much of the Potteries can be seen.

G Force, Drayton Manor Park
This is one of the latest
'white knuckle' rides in this
theme park near Tamworth.
I had to have a go on it.

**Maelstrom,
Drayton Manor Park**
It's all arms and legs in this
graphic image of the ride
in pivotal position.

**Splash Canyon,
Drayton Manor Park**
This picture catches the
moment on the Splash Canyon
boat ride, and some of the
pleasant lakeside
surroundings of the park.

Consall Station, Churnet Valley Railway
This was a great position to view both locomotives and canal boats, in the lovely Churnet Valley,
a thankfully unsung location. The preserved railway runs between Cheddleton and Froghall.

Locomotive 80098 pulling out of Consall Station
This wider view shows the beautiful wooded surroundings of the Churnet Valley.

Mining Monument, Apedale Country Park, the Potteries
This is a monument commemorating all those men who worked underground in mining activities in Staffordshire.

Alton Castle
This Gothic-style castle was designed by Augustus Welby Pugin, of Houses of Parliament fame.
It is on the site of a medieval castle used by one of Richard I's knights,
and is currently a Roman Catholic Youth Retreat with hostel accommodation.

Trader and Dr Johnson's House, Lichfield

The market trader hands a potential sale item to his customer on his Market Square stall in front of the house where Dr Samuel Johnson was born in 1709. The building has been a museum dedicated to the learned man of the eighteenth century since 1901.

128

Tudor House, Lichfield
Now a café, the half-timbered
house was built in 1510.

Gailey Reservoir
The reservoir lies at the junction of the M6 and the A5, but once on its shores, the scenery belies its situation, with rural views taking in Cannock Chase to the east. This view is to the north.

River Churnet at Oakamoor
Yet another section of this fine valley is encountered at Oakamoor.

We're on AIR, Alton Towers
Flying through the air like Superman, the riders' expressions show the exhilaration of
one of Alton Tower's latest white-knuckle adventures.

Nemesis, Alton Towers
Photographing at Alton Towers restricted my time, but I took a ride on Nemesis. The cars seem to do everything at a rate of knots including swooping into and out of a tunnel as seen here.

Croxden Abbey
Cistercian monks arrived to start building an abbey here in 1179, and it took about fifty years to complete.
They bred sheep for their wool, and the place remained untouched until falling into disuse after
the Dissolution of the Monasteries about 1538.

The Pagoda, Alton Towers
The gardens here are a splendid diversion from the theme park's rides, and were created by the
15th Earl of Shrewsbury and his nephew, John Talbot, in the eighteenth and nineteenth centuries.
The pagoda is an exact copy of the To Ho Pagoda in Canton, China.

Fishing at Rudyard Reservoir
A telephoto lens enabled the capture of this image seen at the northern end of the lake.

Towards Three Shires Head
We are looking upstream on the
River Dane towards the
northernmost boundary
of Staffordshire, where it meets
Cheshire and Derbyshire
at the bridge.

Buildings and enclosures near Wetton
When the opportunity arrives, I prefer a design or pattern in a landscape.
The limestone walls and buildings of the White Peak lend themselves perfectly to my quest.

Towards Flash
The highest village in England lies off the A53 Leek to Buxton road at 1518 feet/463 metres.

Froghall Wharf
In the mid nineteenth century, this sylvan setting on the Cauldon Canal in the
Churnet Valley was a hive of industry, as limestone came here from the local
Cauldon quarries to be transported by barge or the nearby railway line.

Narrowboat at the Black Lion (Cauldon Canal), Churnet Valley
Only careful map readers and locals know how to find this location, but given a
good day as seen here, it is as idyllic as you could wish.

Weaver Hills across Churnet Valley
The view is near Thornbury Hall, a short distance from Kingsley Holt.

Alton and the Weaver Hills
Alton's south side is on the slope of a hill and gives views over the town and wooded valley
towards the open Weaver Hills. Note the distinctive architecture of Alton Castle.

Shutlingsloe and cottage
An enigmatic picture to end the book. It was photographed on a
December dawn near the A53, and contains minimal subject matter.